The Really Easy Flute Book

Very first solos for flute with piano accompaniment

selected and edited by Judith Pearce & Christopher Gunning

GW00566289

FABER *ff* MUSIC

2

1. THE PIANIST
Der Pianist

CG/JP

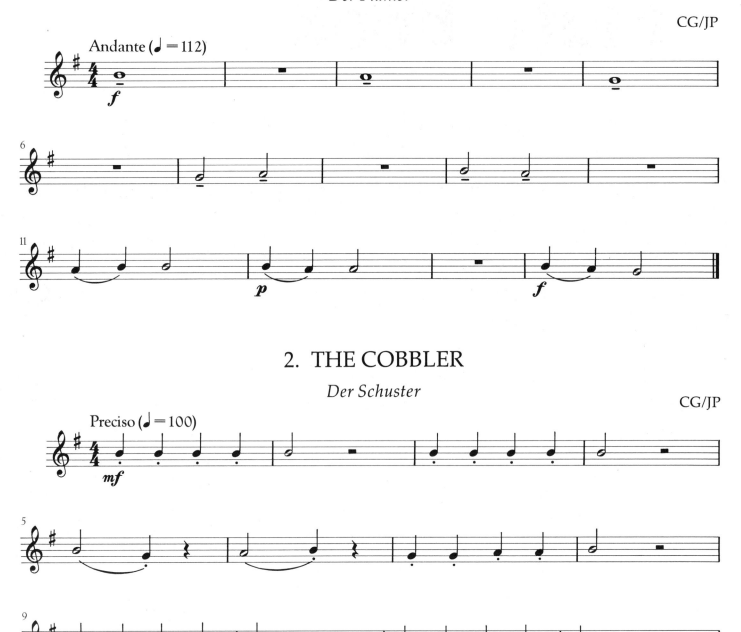

2. THE COBBLER
Der Schuster

CG/JP

3. WILLOWS
Weiden

Gently flowing (♩ = 120)
Weich fliessend

CG/JP

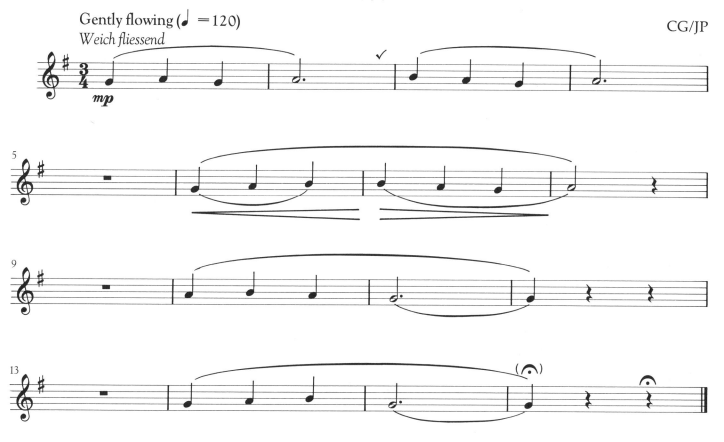

4. DOT TO DOT
Von Punkt zu Punkt

CG/JP

Con delicatezza (♩ = 92)

5. THE BLUEBELL LINE
Die Glockenblumenlinie

CG/JP

6. ARIA
Arie

J. C. Bach
(1735–1782)

7. PUPPETS
Marionetten

CG/JP

8. GLIDING
Gleiten

CG/JP

9. SILVER LAKE
Silberner See

CG/JP

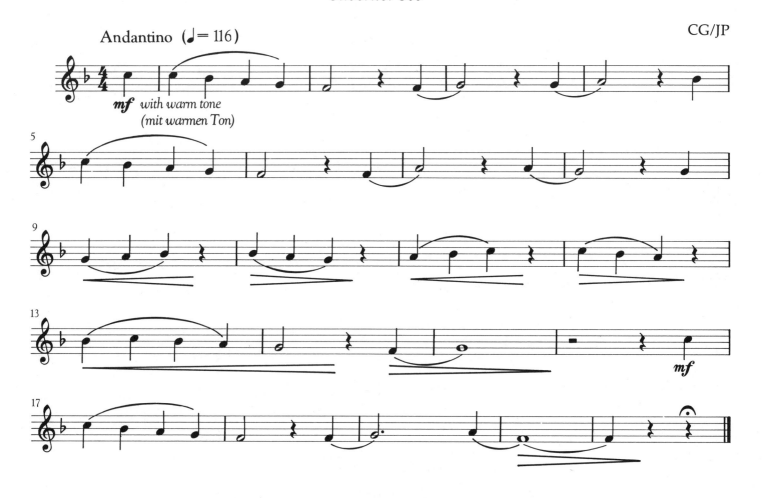

10. LIGHTLY ROW
Mit leichtem Ruderschlag

Trad.

11. SLOVAKIAN HOOP DANCE
Slowakischer Ringtanz

CG/JP

12. ROCKING
Wiegend

CG/JP

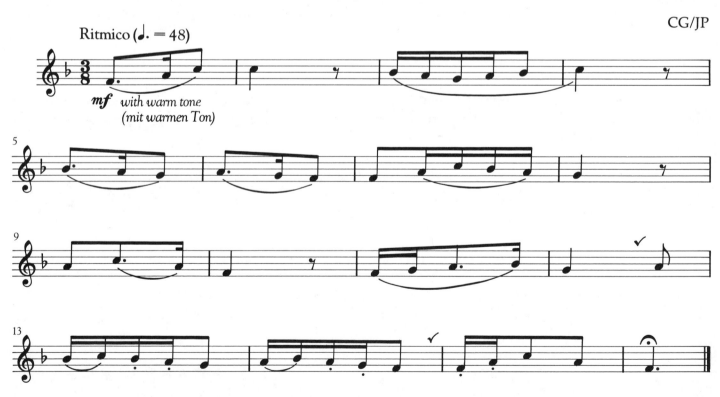

13. AIR FROM 'FIGARO'

Weise aus 'Figaro'

W. A. Mozart
(1756–1791)

14. REFLECTIONS

Spiegelbilden

CG/JP

15. TIBETAN FOLK SONG
Tibetanisches Volkslied

Trad.

16. THE LOVE THAT I HAD
Einstige Liebe

Trad. Mexican

*   May be played an octave higher
    Kann eine Oktave höher gespielt werden

17. WHITE ROSE OF MY HEART

Weiße Rose meines Herzens

Trad. Welsh

18. ELIZABETHAN DANCE

Elisabetanischer Tanz

W. Rosseter
(c1575–1623)

19. THE ROMMELPOT

Der Rommelpot

Trad. Belgian

20. SYRIAN LOVE SONG

Syrisches Liebeslied

Trad.

21. JEU! JEU!

El Salvadorean folk song

The Really Easy Flute Book

Very first solos for flute with piano accompaniment

selected and edited by Judith Pearce & Christopher Gunning

PREFACE

Even though you have just begun learning the flute, you would probably like to play complete pieces. So here is a collection of original compositions and arrangements, starting with your first three notes and progressing gradually as your ability grows.

It is a good idea to take things slowly at first—there is a lot to learn, and patience in mastering the early stages will certainly be rewarded later on.

These pieces are intended to make learning as enjoyable as possible, guiding you through the basic essentials of tone production, articulation and fingering, at the same time always introducing new notes.

Judith Pearce & Christopher Gunning

CONTENTS

© 1987 by Faber Music Ltd
First published in 1987 by Faber Music Ltd
3 Queen Square London WC1N 3AU
Music drawn by Donald Sheppard
Cover illustration by John Levers
Printed in England by Caligraving Ltd
All rights reserved

ISBN 0-571-50881-2

FABER *ff* MUSIC

1. THE PIANIST

Der Pianist

CG/JP

2. THE COBBLER

Der Schuster

CG/JP

3. WILLOWS

Weiden

CG/JP

4. DOT TO DOT
Von Punkt zu Punkt

CG/JP

5. THE BLUEBELL LINE
Die Glockenblumenlinie

CG/JP

6. ARIA

Arie

Flowing (♩. = 42)
Fliessend

J. C. Bach
(1735–1782)

f with full tone, gently tongued
(*mit vollem Ton und leichter Flatterzunge*)

mf

7. PUPPETS
Marionetten

CG/JP

8. GLIDING
Gleiten

CG/JP

9. SILVER LAKE

Silberner See

CG/JP

10. LIGHTLY ROW

Mit leichtem Ruderschlag

Trad.

Variation (♩.= 72)

11. SLOVAKIAN HOOP DANCE

Slowakischer Ringtanz

CG/JP

12. ROCKING
Wiegend

CG/JP

13. AIR FROM 'FIGARO'

Weise aus 'Figaro'

W. A. Mozart
(1756–1791)

14. REFLECTIONS

Spiegelbilden

CG/JP

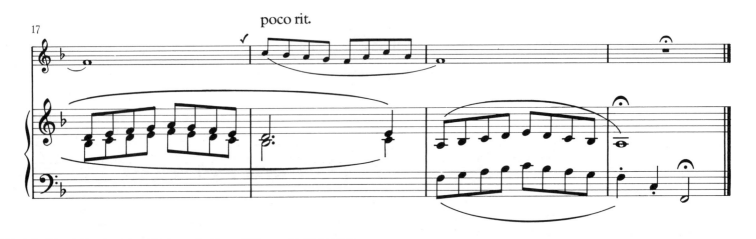

15. TIBETAN FOLK SONG

Tibetanisches Volkslied

Trad.

16. THE LOVE THAT I HAD

Einstige Liebe

Trad. Mexican

* The flute part may be played an octave higher.
Der Flötenteil kann eine Oktave höher gespielt werden.

17. WHITE ROSE OF MY HEART

Weiße Rose meines Herzens

Trad. Welsh

18. ELIZABETHAN DANCE

Elisabetanischer Tanz

W. Rosseter
(*c*1575–1623)

19. THE ROMMELPOT

Der Rommelpot

Trad. Belgian

20. SYRIAN LOVE SONG

Syrisches Liebeslied

Trad.

21. JEU! JEU!

El Salvadorean folk song